# Migration

| Contents | Page |
|---|---|


written by Suzette Toms

# *What is migration?*

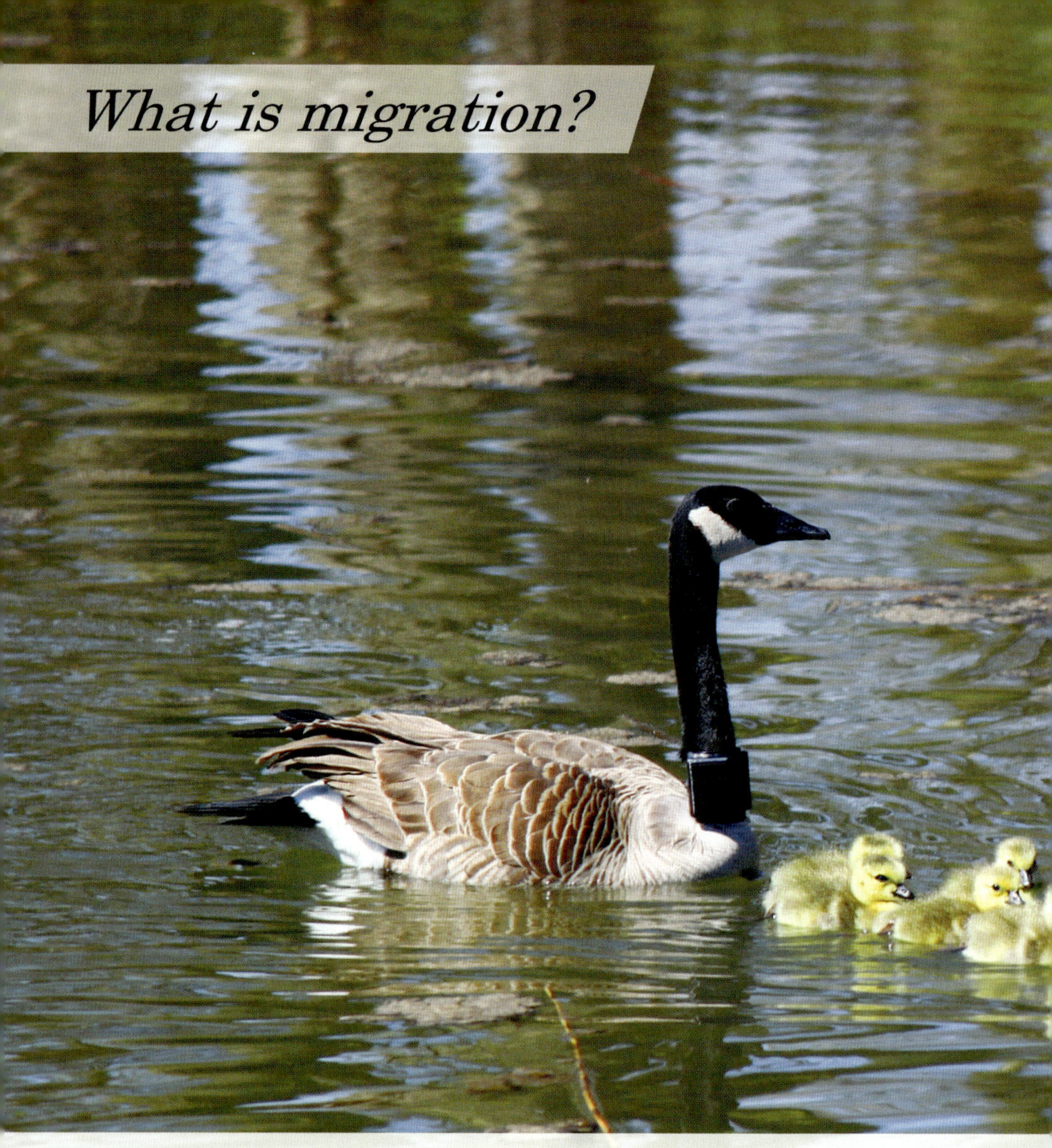

Migration is the movement of people, animals, plants and other living things from one place to another. Not all migrations are the same. Some follow a pattern. Others happen for different reasons, at different times and by different methods.

Animals migrate for one or more of three reasons:

- food and water
- climate changes
- mating and breeding.

Humpback whales travel from their breeding grounds near Hawaii, Japan and Central America to feed on massive schools of krill available in the North Pacific Ocean every summer.

The search for fresh food and water is the reason why zebras cross the Serengeti every year, following the rains which produce new plants for them to eat.

# Climate change

Winter snows and cold weather are why many species of birds fly great distances to reach warmer climates, while other animals travel to special places to shelter from the cold. Little brown bats fly from outdoor roosts used in summer to their winter homes, (safe sheltered caves with even temperatures), to sleep during winter.

# Insect migration

Insects also migrate for seasonal reasons. The Monarch butterfly is famous for flying huge distances from northern parts of America to Mexico to avoid freezing winter temperatures. Not all insects migrate, but many do, including grasshoppers, locusts, dragonflies, leafhoppers, aphids, beetles, and of course, other butterflies and moths.

# Breeding

Many animals migrate to reproduce. They travel to breeding grounds to meet mates and give birth to a new generation.

Emperor penguins trek enormous distances inland across the Antarctic ice to reach their annual breeding grounds.

When it is time to spawn, salmon swim from the middle of the ocean to the exact area of fresh water in the river or stream where they were born.

Migrations take place at different times for different reasons.
Some migrations are regular and happen every year with the change of seasons.

Others might happen only once in a lifetime.

Some animals migrate all the time, following or seeking the best food and water sources. These animals and insects are called 'nomadic' and include most herd animals such as buffalo and African elephants.

# Navigation

How do they know where to go? Animals and insects navigate by many different ways:

- watching for landmarks they remember
- following trails or coastlines
- using their sense of smell
- following the position of the sun or stars
- trusting their instincts.

Some can even feel the magnetic pull of the Earth!

# Immigrants or emigrants?

Human migration has happened throughout history. Over time, moving from place to place has become easier and faster as transport methods have improved. People who migrate into a country are called immigrants, and those leaving a region are called emigrants. Some people choose to emigrate: that means they leave their homes willingly, but there are others who have choices forced upon them: they are unwilling migrants.

FÖDERATION
RUSS
Ochots-
kisches
Kamtsch
Meer
Untere Tunguska
Aldan
Lena
Ulan-Bator
MONGOLEI
Baikalsee
Amur
Angara
Ob
Jenissej
Irtysch
Volga
Kama
Peking
DEMOKR
VOLKSR
KOREA
Pjöngjang
Seoul
REP.
KOREA
CHINA
Huang He
OSPI
LSK
EUROPÄISCHE UNION
BUNDESREPUBLIK
DEUTSCHLAND
Hanoi
Hainan
LAOS
Vientiane
VIETNAM
THAILAND
Südchinesi
REISEPASS
Bangkok
KAMBOD-
SCHA
Phnom
Penh
BRU
Band
Kuala
Lumpur
Seri Begawa
MALAYS
Singapur
SINGAPUR
Sumatra
Jakar
Jav
Cocos -In.
(austr.)
Christ
(austr.)
MOSAMBIK
Kanal v. Mo
aputo
DISCHE
Südlicher Wendekreis
mbabane
VASILAND
O
ZEAN
Amsterdam
(frz.)
St-Paul
(frz.)
Crozet-In.
(frz.)
Prinz-Edward-In.
(südafr.)
Kerguelen
(frz.)

# Push or pull?

Willing migrants decide to travel from their home to find:

- new job opportunities
- better living conditions
- safe medical care
- good education.

These are called 'pull factors'.

Unwilling migrants are people forced to leave their homes because of 'push factors' – slavery, war, famine or drought make them become refugees.

Natural disasters such as earthquakes, floods, volcanic eruptions and storms can also force people to migrate. Finding out why people migrate helps us to understand our history.

# Plant migration

Plants don't migrate in the same way humans and animals do, but their 'movement' is also described as migration. New plants need space to grow in other places to avoid overcrowding, so the seeds are taken away from the parent plants, carried by wind, water, birds, animals or humans. Examples are: coconuts floating away on water; fruit eaten by birds; seeds catching on the fur or hair of animals; by people on their shoes or clothes, or on the wheels of vehicles. Many nuts and fruits drop to the ground then roll away. Some plants have pods which explode and throw their seeds out. Others are blown by the wind.
How well and far seeds can spread!

# Future trends

When we look at migration patterns we discover some very interesting facts – about the natural world and our human world and how they are connected.

Migration patterns give us clues about:

- our history
- our current living conditions
- our environment.

This information can help us predict future trends.